Amazing Animals
Penguins

Dave Whitfield

WEIGL PUBLISHERS INC.

Published by Weigl Publishers Inc.
350 5th Avenue, Suite 3304, PMB 6G
New York, NY 10118-0069

Amazing Animals series ©2009
WEIGL PUBLISHERS INC. www.weigl.com

Library of Congress Cataloging-in-
Publication Data

Whitfield, David.
  Penguins / Dave Whitfield.
     p. cm. – (Amazing animals)
  Includes index.
  ISBN 978-1-59036-968-5 (hard cover :
alk. paper) – ISBN 978-1-59036-969-2
(soft cover : alk. paper)
  1. Penguins–Juvenile literature. I. Title.
  QL696.S473W47 2008
  598.47–dc22

2008003787

Editor
Heather Kissock
Design and Layout
Terry Paulhus,
Kathryn Livingstone

Photograph Credits
Every reasonable effort has been made
to trace ownership and to obtain
permission to reprint copyright material.
The publishers would be pleased to have
any errors or omissions brought to their
attention so that they may be corrected
in subsequent printings.

All photos supplied by Getty Images.

Printed in the United States of America
1 2 3 4 5 6 7 8 9 0 12 11 10 09 08

About This Book

This book tells you all about penguins. Find out where they live and what they eat. Discover how you can help to protect them. You can also read about them in myths and legends from around the world.

Words in **bold** are explained in the Words to Know section at the back of the book.

Useful Websites

Addresses in this book take you to the home pages of websites that have information about penguins.

All of the Internet URLs given in the book were valid at the time of publication. However, due to the dynamic nature of the Internet, some addresses may have changed, or sites may have ceased to exist since publication. While the author and publisher regret any inconvenience this may cause readers, no responsibility for any such changes can be accepted by either the author or the publisher.

Contents

Meet the Penguin

Penguins are seabirds that cannot fly. They have mostly black and white feathers.

Penguins are **carnivores**. They spend much of their time underwater, hunting for food. When penguins dive into the ocean to hunt, they swim by flapping their wings. Penguins can swim at speeds up to 15 miles (24.1 kilometers) per hour.

▼ Penguins often swim and feed in groups.

The Penguin Family

- There are 17 types of penguins.
- The largest penguin is the emperor penguin, which weighs up to 90 pounds (41 kilograms) and stands almost 4 feet (1.2 meters) tall.
- The smallest is the fairy penguin. It is about 16 inches tall (41 centimeters) and weighs 2 pounds (1 kg).

▲ Penguins stand upright and waddle when they walk.

A Very Special Animal

Most penguins live in cold regions. To stay warm in cold climates, penguins have a layer of fat under their skin called blubber.

Penguin feathers are designed to keep the penguins warm. Close to their body, they have **down** feathers. Over the down feathers, they have waterproof feathers. These feathers overlap so that wind cannot get through to their skin.

▼ Penguins often huddle in big groups to keep each other warm.

A penguin's bill is used to catch food.

Waterproof feathers cover a penguin's body and help the penguin keep warm.

A penguin's body is **streamlined** for swimming.

Short, strong legs and webbed feet help the penguin move in water.

Penguins have a short, wedge-shaped tail that they use to steer through the water.

Keeping It Together

Penguins are social birds. They mainly live in groups. During the breeding season, some penguins live in rookeries on the shore. Rookeries are groups in which penguins mate, nest, and raise their chicks.

When penguins find a mate, they touch each other's neck and beak. They sing to each other so they can know each other's voices. Penguin mates stay together for as long as they have chicks.

▶ Rookeries can have hundreds of thousands of penguins and cover large areas of land.

Penguin Talk

Penguins use three types of calls to talk to each other.

- A contact call helps penguins recognize each other.

- A display call is used between partners.

- A threat call warns others of danger.

How Penguins Eat

Penguins eat fish, squid, and **krill**. To catch this food, penguins dive into the water and swim. Their wings act like flippers. Penguins flap their wings in order to "fly" after **prey**.

A penguin's bill has a hook in the end to help the penguin grab its food. Bristles on the penguin's tongue make sure slippery seafood does not get away. When a penguin catches its prey, it swallows the food whole.

▼ Penguins usually stay underwater for less than one minute.

What a Meal!

- Penguins drink salt water from the ocean. Their bodies are able to remove the salt from the water. The salt is pushed out grooves in their bill.

- A penguin does not always find its food in the ocean. Sometimes, it finds food by searching openings in the ice.

▲ Krill swim in large groups called swarms.

Where Penguins Live

All penguins live in the **Southern Hemisphere**. This includes the continents of Africa, Antarctica, Australia, and South America. The Southern Hemisphere has different climates. Some penguins live in hot countries near the **equator**. Others live on the cold pack ice of Antarctica.

Penguins live on islands and remote areas. They are found near the ocean in places where there are few land **predators**.

▼ The erect-crested penguin lives in the warm climate of New Zealand.

Penguin Range

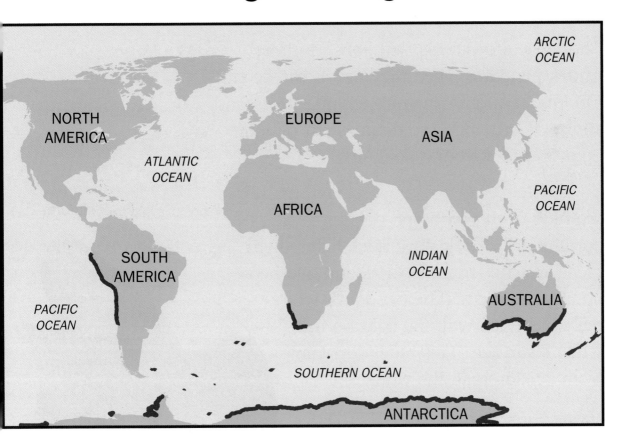

NORTH AMERICA

EUROPE

ASIA

ARCTIC OCEAN

ATLANTIC OCEAN

AFRICA

PACIFIC OCEAN

SOUTH AMERICA

INDIAN OCEAN

PACIFIC OCEAN

AUSTRALIA

SOUTHERN OCEAN

ANTARCTICA

N
W E
S

| 0 | 1,000 | 2,000 km |
| 0 | 622 | 1,243 mi |

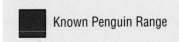

Known Penguin Range

Friends and Enemies

Sharks, leopard seals, sea lions, and orcas attack penguins when they are in the ocean. On land, penguin enemies include foxes and snakes. Large birds sometimes eat penguin eggs or attack young penguins.

To hide from predators, penguins use **camouflage**. Their dark back helps them blend in with water. Birds flying overhead cannot see them. The penguin's white belly blends in with the light on the water's surface. This hides penguins from predators in the water.

▼ Leopard seals are known to be fierce predators.

Useful Websites

http://library.thinkquest.org/ CR02I5022/animals.htm

Go to this website to learn more about the other animals that live with penguins.

Living with Penguins

There are many different animals that live in the same places as penguins.

- seals
- orcas
- squid
- krill
- foxes
- snakes

▲ Southern elephant seals mainly eat fish and squid but have been known to feed on penguins as well.

Growing Up

Penguins usually lay one or two eggs in their nest. The parents then take turns keeping the eggs warm.

When a chick hatches, it calls to its parents so they know its voice. This helps the parents find their chick when they return from hunting. Adult penguins will feed only their own chick.

Young chicks are covered with down feathers. The feathers are not waterproof, so chicks cannot go into the water. After the waterproof feathers grow, chicks can go in the water to swim and find their own food.

▼ Adult penguins take turns feeding their chick.

Growth Chart

Penguin eggs range in size depending on the type of penguin. Some can be up to 5 inches (13 cm) in length.

A newborn penguin chick can be up to 6 inches (15 cm) in height.

A chick leaves its parents when its waterproof feathers grow. This happens when the chick is between 7 weeks and 13 months of age.

▲ In nature, penguins live for about 15 to 20 years.

Under Threat

Long ago, people used penguins for food and clothing. In the 1800s and 1900s, penguins were killed for the oil in their fat layers.

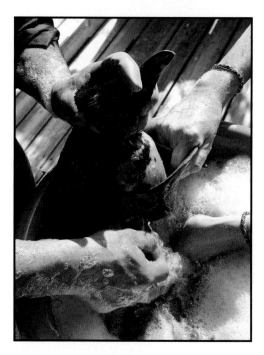

▼ After an oil spill, rescue teams try to save birds by bathing them to remove oil.

Today, pollution is the penguin's greatest threat. Penguins have died because they have become trapped in debris that is floating in the ocean. Oil spills also hurt penguins. When penguins are soaked in oil, their feathers lose their waterproofing. The birds cannot stay warm.

Useful Websites

www.penguins.cl

Visit this website to learn how people are trying to save penguins.

▲ Penguins in tropical climates often share their territory with humans. This can affect the penguin's way of life.

What Do You Think?

Overfishing of krill is a great threat to penguins. When humans take too many krill for themselves, penguins go hungry. If penguins go hungry or cannot nest properly, fewer penguins will be born. Do you think overfishing should be stopped? Can the problem be solved in another way?

Myths and Legends

There are few myths about penguins. This is because most penguins do not live near people. Some penguins can be found in southern Australia. It is believed that one myth about penguins came from the **Aboriginal Peoples** there.

In the myth, two penguins escort a whale named Jeedara to a stone table in an Australian cove. There, they meet with other Australian animals. Following the meeting, the penguins take Jeedara back to his home. Other animals are not as lucky. They turn into stone.

▶ Aboriginal Australians use myths to explain the origins of the world and the events that happen in it.

Several movies have been made about penguins. *Happy Feet* is a cartoon about a penguin who cannot sing. Penguins need to be able to sing to find their true love, but Mumble, the movie's star, is a great tap dancer instead.

March of the Penguins is a **documentary**. It follows penguins in Antarctica as they take a long journey through blizzards and dangerous water to find the perfect mate.

▶ Penguins helped other animals escape from a zoo in the 2005 movie *Madagascar*.

Quiz

1. How many types of penguin are there?
   (a) **10** (b) **17** (c) **25**

2. Where do penguins live?
   (a) **Northern Hemisphere** (b) **North Pole**
   (c) **Southern Hemisphere**

3. What do penguins eat?
   (a) **seafood** (b) **plants** (c) **insects**

4. How many types of calls does a penguin
   use to communicate?
   (a) **2** (b) **3** (c) **4**

5. Which of these animals attacks penguins?
   (a) **lions** (b) **bears** (c) **leopard seals**

Answers:
1. (b) There are 17 types of penguin.
2. (c) Penguins live in the Southern Hemisphere.
3. (a) Penguins eat seafood, such as krill and fish.
4. (b) Penguins use three types of calls to talk to each other.
5. (c) Leopard seals attack penguins.

Find out More

To find out more about penguins, visit the websites in this book. You can also write to these organizations.

Organization for the Conservation of Penguins
Casilla 263
Punta Arenas, Chile

Southern African Foundation for the Conservation of Coastal Birds
P.O. Box 11116
Bloubergrant
Cape Town
7443
South Africa

World Wildlife Fund
1250 24th Street NW
Washington, DC 20037

Words to Know

Aboriginal Peoples
original inhabitants of an area
camouflage
a feature that helps an animal
hide in its environment
carnivores
animals that eat meat
documentary
a movie that is based on real events
down
small, soft feathers

equator
an imaginary line around Earth that
divides it into north and south
krill
tiny, shrimp-like animals
predators
animals that hunt other animals for food
prey
animals that are hunted by other animals
Southern Hemisphere
the southern part of Earth
streamlined
shaped to allow smooth travel
through water

Index